Journeying
Through the Days 2012

A Calendar and Journal for Personal Reflection

JOURNEYING THROUGH THE DAYS 2012®
A Calendar and Journal for Personal Reflection
Copyright © 2011 by Upper Room Books®. All rights reserved.

No part of this book may be used or reproduced in any manner whatsoever without written permission of the publisher except in the case of brief quotations embodied in critical articles or reviews. For information, write Upper Room Books, 1908 Grand Avenue, Nashville, TN 37212.

UPPER ROOM®, UPPER ROOM BOOKS®, and design logos are trademarks owned by The Upper Room®, a Ministry of GBOD®, Nashville, Tennessee. All rights reserved.

The Upper Room Web site: www.upperroom.org

Scripture quotations marked CEB are from the Common English Bible. Copyright © 2010 Common English Bible. Used by permission.

Scripture quotations marked GNT are from the Good News Translation in Today's English Version—Second Edition. Copyright © 1992 by American Bible Society. Used by permission. All rights reserved.

Scripture quotations designated KJV are from the King James Version of the Bible.

Scripture quotations marked THE MESSAGE are from *THE MESSAGE*. Copyright © by Eugene H. Peterson 1993, 1994, 1995, 1996, 2000, 2001, 2002. Used by permission of NavPress Publishing Group.

Scripture quotations marked NIV are taken from the Holy Bible, New International Version®, NIV®. Copyright © 1973, 1978, 1984 by Biblica, Inc.™ Used by permission of Zondervan. All rights reserved worldwide.

Scripture quotations marked NJB are taken from *The New Jerusalem Bible*, copyright © 1985 by Darton, Longman & Todd, Ltd. and Doubleday, a division of Random House, Inc. Reprinted by Permission.

Scripture quotations marked NLT are taken from the Holy Bible, New Living Translation, copyright © 1996, 2004, 2007. Used by permission of Tyndale House Publishers, Inc., Carol Stream, Illinois 60188. All rights reserved.

Scripture quotations marked NRSV are from the New Revised Standard Version of the Bible, © copyright 1989, National Council of the Churches of Christ in the United States of America. Used by permission. All rights reserved.

Scripture selections for each day are chosen from *The Revised Common Lectionary* copyright © 1992 Consultation on Common Texts. Used by permission.

At the time of publication all Web sites referenced in this book were valid. However, due to the fluid nature of the internet some addresses may have changed or the content may no longer be relevant.

ISBN 978-0-8358-1049-4

Cover and interior photographs: Copyright © Rev. brotherjohn Gaudreau, OEF.
Cover and interior design: Left Coast Design, Portland, OR / www.lcoast.com
Interior implementation: PerfecType, Nashville, TN
First printing: 2011

Printed in the United States of America

Journaling: Connecting to Yourself and to God

Leisa A. Hammett

The whirl and drone of machines, the noisy play of children, the demands of bosses, the hammering staccato of noise—loud noise, white noise, the noise of critical commentary and to-do lists swimming in our heads—so infuses our daily lives that we have forgotten we have a choice: we can choose to disconnect from the world's chatter. Disconnecting from the noise allows us to plug back into our quiet selves and to reconnect with God. Our souls, our minds, our bodies all crave connection, and daily journaling provides that connection.

Give yourself permission to listen: What are your body and your spirit telling you they need most? For what are you hungry, or hurting, or grateful? What needs the catharsis of spilling out through words onto paper?

There's a reason so many therapists, self-help publications, and writers recommend journaling. There's something healing about "talking" to ourselves on the page. Journaling can be a form of spiritual exercise and practice, a "de-stressor." We may just sit down to make a to-do list when out from the recessed, dark, cobwebbed corners of our consciousness comes a revelation, a truth, something we need to hear. A missing piece to a puzzle in our lives . . . once we become silent, pen in hand, page before us.

Because journaling has become increasingly popular in our culture, we sometimes associate an expectation with the practice, such as: "It *must* be done daily!" And there have been months in my adult life, during the last thirty years, when I have not journaled. But eventually, a crisis, a challenging circumstance, a complex and even a happy dilemma has beckoned me back to the page. Pen to paper. The answers come.

I believe the Divine can commune with humankind in many ways and sometimes it can be through the process of journaling thoughts on a page.

Abandon rigidity with your journaling. There is no right way or wrong way. You may find that you prefer a certain pen—how it touches the paper and how the ink flows. Or, that may not matter to you. You can start writing something and leave it in midsentence as another thought enters your mind. Perhaps that interrupting thought is more important—something urgent, needing to reveal itself onto paper. Your journal is yours. There are no grades and no teachers—except you, the practice, your journal, and the delight of what it may reveal and teach you.

My favorite time of day for this connection to self and to the Divine is morning. Much has been written about the process of "mind dumping," a cleansing ritual where we can dump our thoughts, fears, worries—the mental clutter onto the page. There it goes. Sometimes clumsily and randomly. Out it pours.

My journaling is often spontaneous and particular to a given day. What needs to be said that day? What's bothering me? What's delighting me? Is there something that I wish to figure out? The paper sits hungry and anxious, eagerly listening and waiting to reflect back when given the chance. Sometimes my daily dumping or journaling ritual takes the form of a list. I purge the tornadic thoughts of my mind and connect them to the page—ousting my noisy stream of mental chatter.

Sometimes I journal at night or in the middle of the day, especially when an issue needles my mental energy. Journaling at night can be a way to clear my mind for a peaceful night's sleep. Incorporating a to-do list at night, or in the morning—even as I sit down at my desk to work—is another way I can jump-start a productive day.

Almost always I incorporate my daily gratitude practice into my journaling—listing at least five things for which I am grateful. The list can be as simple as gratitude expressed for yummy morning mocha, my walk along the lakeside, the kiss of a loved one, the sunshine through my windows, the heat warming me. When I take time to say Thanks, gratitude resonates within me and perspective fills my heart, even when life seems oh so less than perfect. Through gratitude, I realize that despite current challenges I am blessed. Blessed simply and abundantly with the Gift of Life.

Sometimes I include affirmations in my journal: What in my life do I want to affirm? To create, to cocreate with the creator? It may be to have a loving attitude toward a coworker whom I find troublesome. It may be to have a productive day. Affirmations can jump-start a positive mental attitude. In an often-negative world, affirmations help to infuse my spirit with the positive, hopeful, and good. Affirmations are a form of prayer, and journaling can be a prayer to God, a dialogue about the good, the bad, and the ugly. I believe God has a large complaint department that "can deal," and also a Big Band to celebrate life's joys as well.

At times I dissect my night's dreams in my journal. Some people believe God speaks to us through our dreams. I scribble down those dreams and the effect can be the same as journaling about other matters—answers that sometimes I don't know I am looking for then surprise and delight.

Journaling can be a document of life. Some people collect quotes in their journals. Sometimes, I write scenes for a possible novel.

In my life, journaling has become like exercise and eating well to support my body, mind, and soul. My perfect morning routine consists of several minutes practicing yoga, several minutes of journaling (for as little as five but as long as thirty minutes), and several minutes of meditation, (sitting in silence with my eyes closed, again for a little as five but as long as thirty minutes). Yoga awakens my body. Journaling cleanses my mind. Meditation settles both. Only then am I ready to meet my day. At some point during the day, I'll take a walk in nature and maybe lift some hand weights. I support all these practices by eating pure food, as close to nature as God created.

I find that if I do not follow this routine (including journaling), at some point I will become cranky and stiff—mentally, spiritually, physically. My mind crams with negative chatter. All these practices, including journaling, truly are a part of my daily mental health plan.

What a simple yet abundant gift is journaling. I invite you to make the time and give your spirit a few moments of connecting with yourself and God daily through journaling.

The healing practice of journaling has buoyed author, speaker, and advocate, Leisa A. Hammett not only through the loss of her job, the diagnosis of her only child with autism, and a divorce, but also through many joyous celebrations and gifts—big and small—of daily life. A veteran communicator and published magazine and newspaper writer, she is the author and producer of From Heartache to Hope: Middle Tennessee Families Living with Autism *and blogs at www.LeisaHammett.com.*

Never lose an opportunity of seeing anything beautiful, for beauty is God's handwriting.

RALPH WALDO EMERSON

SUNDAY · JANUARY 1

NEW YEAR'S DAY

The one who was seated on the throne said, "See, I am making all things new."

Revelation 21:5, NRSV

ECCLESIASTES 3:1-13 · PSALM 8
REVELATION 21:1-6a · MATTHEW 25:31-46

MONDAY · JANUARY 2

> The voice of the LORD is heard on the seas;
> the glorious God thunders,
> and his voice echoes over the ocean.
>
> Psalm 29:3, GNT

TUESDAY · JANUARY 3

> All of Judea, including all the people of Jerusalem, went out to see and hear John. And when they confessed their sins, he baptized them in the Jordan River.
>
> Mark 1:5, NLT

WEDNESDAY · JANUARY 4

Paul said to some disciples at Ephesus, "Did you receive the Holy Spirit when you believed? Did you take God into your mind only, or did you also embrace him with your heart?"

Acts 19:2, THE MESSAGE

THURSDAY · JANUARY 5

The LORD gives strength to his people and blesses them with peace.

Psalm 29:11, GNT

FRIDAY · JANUARY 6

EPIPHANY OF THE LORD

When God began to create the heavens and the earth—the earth was without shape or form, it was dark over the deep sea, and God's wind swept over the waters—God said, "Let there be light." And so light appeared.

Genesis 1:1-3, CEB

SATURDAY · JANUARY 7

John the Baptist said, "After me will come one more powerful than I, the thongs of whose sandals I am not worthy to stoop down and untie."

Mark 1:7, NIV

When you know how much God is in love with you then you can only live your life radiating that love.

MOTHER TERESA

SUNDAY · JANUARY 8

BAPTISM OF THE LORD

John the Baptist said, "I have baptized you with water, but [Jesus Christ] will baptize you with the Holy Spirit."

Mark 1:8, NJB

GENESIS 1:1-5 · PSALM 29
ACTS 19:1-7 · MARK 1:4-11

MONDAY · JANUARY 9

Don't you know that your body is a temple of the Holy Spirit who is in you? Don't you know that you have the Holy Spirit from God?

1 Corinthians 6:19, CEB

TUESDAY · JANUARY 10

It was you [LORD] who formed my
    inward parts;
you knit me together in my mother's
    womb.

Psalm 139:13, NRSV

WEDNESDAY · JANUARY 11

Eli told Samuel, "Go and lie down, and if [the LORD] calls you, say, 'Speak, LORD, for your servant is listening.'"

1 Samuel 3:9, NIV

THURSDAY · JANUARY 12

Jesus decided to go to Galilee. He found Philip and said to him, "Follow me."

John 1:43, NRSV

FRIDAY · JANUARY 13

Philip went and found Nathanael and told him, "We've found the One Moses wrote of in the Law, the One preached by the prophets. It's *Jesus*, Joseph's son, the one from Nazareth!"

John 1:45, THE MESSAGE

SATURDAY · JANUARY 14

"Can anything good come from Nazareth?" Nathanael asked. "Come and see," answered Philip.

John 1:46, GNT

Jesus calls us to be grateful for every moment that we have lived and to claim our unique journey as God's way to mold our hearts to greater conformity with God's own.

HENRI J. M. NOUWEN

© REV. BROTHERJOHN GAUDREAU OEF. ALL RIGHTS RESERVED.

SUNDAY · JANUARY 15

> O LORD, you have examined my heart
> and know everything about me. . . .
> You see me when I travel
> and when I rest at home.
> You know everything I do.
>
> Psalm 139:1, 3, NLT

1 SAMUEL 3:1-10 (11-20) · PSALM 139:1-6, 13-18
1 CORINTHIANS 6:12-20 · JOHN 1:43-51

MONDAY · JANUARY 16

> Trust in God at all times, my people.
> Tell him all your troubles,
> for he is our refuge.
>
> Psalm 62:8, GNT

TUESDAY · JANUARY 17

> [God] changed his mind and did not punish [Nineveh] as he had said he would.
>
> Jonah 3:10, GNT

WEDNESDAY · JANUARY 18

Jesus came to Galilee, proclaiming the good news of God, and saying, "The time is fulfilled, and the kingdom of God has come near; repent, and believe in the good news."
Mark 1:14-15, NRSV

THURSDAY · JANUARY 19

[God] alone protects and saves me;
   he is my defender,
   and I shall never be defeated.
Psalm 62:6, GNT

FRIDAY · JANUARY 20

Jesus said to Simon and Andrew, "Come, follow me . . . and I'll show you how to fish for people."

Mark 1:17, CEB

SATURDAY · JANUARY 21

[Jesus] made the same offer [to James and John]. Immediately, they left their father Zebedee, the boat, and the hired hands, and followed.

Mark 1:20, THE MESSAGE

A soulful approach to life allows us to take our time figuring things out. Not having immediate answers is quite all right.

FATHER PAUL KEENAN

© REV. BROTHERJOHN GAUDREAU OEF. ALL RIGHTS RESERVED.

SUNDAY · JANUARY 22

Let all that I am wait quietly before
God,
for my hope is in him.

Psalm 62:5, NLT

JONAH 3:1-5, 10 · PSALM 62:5-12
1 CORINTHIANS 7:29-31 · MARK 1:14-20

MONDAY · JANUARY 23

Anyone who loves God is known by [God].

1 Corinthians 8:3, NRSV

TUESDAY · JANUARY 24

The LORD says, "If anyone does not listen to my words that the prophet speaks in my name, I myself will call him to account."

Deuteronomy 18:19, NIV

WEDNESDAY · JANUARY 25

> While knowledge puffs up, love is what builds up.
>
> 1 Corinthians 8:1, NJB

THURSDAY · JANUARY 26

> The way to become wise is to honor the LORD;
> he gives sound judgment to all who obey his commands.
>
> Psalm 111:10, GNT

FRIDAY · JANUARY 27

They were astounded at [Jesus'] teaching, for he taught them as one having authority, and not as the scribes.

Mark 1:22, NRSV

SATURDAY · JANUARY 28

How amazing are the deeds of the LORD!
All who delight in him should ponder them.

Psalm 111:2, NLT

In our search for the holy, there are times when our restless preparations smother the very truth for which we are searching. We decorate our rooms and make elaborate preparations for our prayer, when a single flower and a moment of waiting are all we need to meet the One Who Comes.

MACRINA WIEDERKEHR

SUNDAY · JANUARY 29

They were all amazed, and they kept on asking one another, "What is this? A new teaching—with authority! He commands even the unclean spirits, and they obey him."

Mark 1:27, NRSV

MONDAY · JANUARY 30

Don't you know? Haven't you heard?
The LORD is the everlasting God;
   he created all the world.

Isaiah 40:28, GNT

TUESDAY · JANUARY 31

Paul wrote, "When I preach the gospel, I cannot boast, for I am compelled to preach. Woe to me if I do not preach the gospel!"

1 Corinthians 9:16, NIV

WEDNESDAY · FEBRUARY 1

How great is our Lord! His power is absolute!
His understanding is beyond comprehension!

Psalm 147:5, NLT

THURSDAY · FEBRUARY 2

Those who trust in the LORD for help will find their strength renewed.
They will rise on wings like eagles.

Isaiah 40:31, GNT

FRIDAY · FEBRUARY 3

In the morning, long before dawn, [Jesus] got up and left the house and went off to a lonely place and prayed there.

Mark 1:35, NJB

SATURDAY · FEBRUARY 4

Paul wrote, "I've become just about every sort of servant there is in my attempts to lead those I meet into a God-saved life."

1 Corinthians 9:22, THE MESSAGE

Miracles . . . rest not so much upon faces or voices or healing power coming suddenly near to us from afar off, but upon our perceptions being made finer, so that for a moment our eyes can see and our ears can hear what is there about us always.

WILLA CATHER

SUNDAY · FEBRUARY 5

Jesus said, "Let us go on to the neighboring towns, so that I may proclaim the message there also; for that is what I came out to do."
Mark 1:38, NRSV

ISAIAH 40:21-31 · PSALM 147:1-11, 20c
1 CORINTHIANS 9:16-23 · MARK 1:29-39

MONDAY · FEBRUARY 6

Naaman went down to the Jordan, dipped himself in it seven times, as Elisha had instructed, and he was completely cured.

2 Kings 5:14, GNT

TUESDAY · FEBRUARY 7

A man with a skin disease approached Jesus, fell to his knees, and begged, "If you want, you can make me clean."

Mark 1:40, CEB

WEDNESDAY · FEBRUARY 8

> To you, O Lord, I called;
> to the Lord I cried for mercy.
>
> Psalm 30:8, NIV

THURSDAY · FEBRUARY 9

> Moved with compassion, Jesus reached out and touched [the leper]. "I am willing," [Jesus] said. "Be healed!"
>
> Mark 1:41, NLT

FRIDAY · FEBRUARY 10

I'm about to burst with song;
 I can't keep quiet about you.
God, my God,
 I can't thank you enough.

Psalm 30:12, THE MESSAGE

SATURDAY · FEBRUARY 11

Surely you know that many runners take part in a race, but only one of them wins the prize. Run, then, in such a way as to win the prize.

1 Corinthians 9:24, GNT

MY GOD AND MY ALL! These words are enough for those who understand, and for those who love, it is a joy to repeat them often. For when you are present, all things are delightful. When you are absent, all things become loathsome. It is you who give a heart tranquility, great peace, and festive joy. . . . O Light eternal, surpassing all created brightness, flash forth the lightning from above and enlighten the inmost recesses of my heart. Cleanse, cheer, enlighten, and enliven my spirit with all its powers, that it may cling to you in ecstasies of joy.

THOMAS À KEMPIS

© REV. BROTHERJOHN GAUDREAU OEF. ALL RIGHTS RESERVED.

SUNDAY · FEBRUARY 12

> Sing to the LORD, you saints of his;
> praise his holy name.
>
> Psalm 30:4, NIV

2 KINGS 5:1-14 · PSALM 30
1 CORINTHIANS 9:24-27 · MARK 1:40-45

MONDAY · FEBRUARY 13

Elijah said to Elisha, "Tell me what I may do for you, before I am taken from you." Elisha said, "Please let me inherit a double share of your spirit."

2 Kings 2:9, NRSV

TUESDAY · FEBRUARY 14

The God who said, "Out of darkness the light shall shine!" is the same God who made his light shine in our hearts.

2 Corinthians 4:6, GNT

WEDNESDAY · FEBRUARY 15

Then let the heavens proclaim his justice,
for God himself will be the judge.

Psalm 50:6, NLT

THURSDAY · FEBRUARY 16

From the cloud there came a voice, "This is my Son, the Beloved. Listen to him."

Mark 9:7, NJB

FRIDAY · FEBRUARY 17

Paul wrote, "If our Message is obscure to anyone, it's not because we're holding back in any way. No, it's because these other people are looking or going the wrong way."

2 Corinthians 4:3, THE MESSAGE

SATURDAY · FEBRUARY 18

The mighty one, God the LORD,
  speaks and summons the earth
  from the rising of the sun to its
    setting.

Psalm 50:1, NRSV

Ah, dear Jesus! I feel the ashes of mortality upon my heart. Give me, please, the courage to acknowledge them; then give me the faithful sight to see them on your forehead; for you have died the death in my stead, my redeemer and my Lord! Amen.

WALTER WANGERIN JR.

SUNDAY · FEBRUARY 19

TRANSFIGURATION SUNDAY

Jesus took Peter, James, and John and led them up a high mountain. His appearance changed from the inside out, right before their eyes.

Mark 9:2, THE MESSAGE

2 KINGS 2:1-12 · PSALM 50:1-6
2 CORINTHIANS 4:3-6 · MARK 9:2-9

MONDAY · FEBRUARY 20

God said to Noah and his family, "With these words I make my covenant with you: I promise that never again will all living beings be destroyed by a flood."

Genesis 9:11, GNT

TUESDAY · FEBRUARY 21

God said, "When I gather the clouds over the earth and the bow appears in the clouds, I shall recall my covenant between myself and you and every living creature."

Genesis 9:14-15, NJB

WEDNESDAY · FEBRUARY 22

ASH WEDNESDAY

The sacrifice acceptable to God is a
broken spirit;
a broken and contrite heart, O God,
you will not despise.

Psalm 51:17, NRSV

THURSDAY · FEBRUARY 23

Unto thee, O Lord, do I lift up my
soul. O my God, I trust in thee.

Psalm 25:1-2, KJV

FRIDAY · FEBRUARY 24

It was by the Spirit that [Christ] went to preach to the spirits in prison. In the past, these spirits were disobedient—when God patiently waited during the time of Noah.

1 Peter 3:19-20, CEB

SATURDAY · FEBRUARY 25

As Jesus came up out of the water... a voice from heaven said, "You are my dearly loved Son, and you bring me great joy."

Mark 1:10-11, NLT

God does not wait for us to make the first move. Even as we sleep, the Spirit works in our lives to arouse us from our slumber. Countless acts of mercy, love, and grace surround us day in and day out. God attempts to get our attention in events, through the influence of other people, in sign-acts of love in the church. But most importantly, God wakes us up by coming to us in the person of Jesus Christ.

PAUL WESLEY CHILCOTE

© REV. BROTHERJOHN GAUDREAU OEF. ALL RIGHTS RESERVED.

SUNDAY · FEBRUARY 26

FIRST SUNDAY IN LENT

Jesus has the last word on everything and everyone, from angels to armies. He's standing right alongside God, and what he says goes.

1 Peter 3:22, THE MESSAGE

GENESIS 9:8-17 · PSALM 25:1-10
1 PETER 3:18-22 · MARK 1:9-15

MONDAY · FEBRUARY 27

It was not through law that Abraham and his offspring received the promise that he would be heir of the world, but through the righteousness that comes by faith.

Romans 4:13, NIV

TUESDAY · FEBRUARY 28

From the four corners of the earth people are coming to their senses, are running back to GOD.

Psalm 22:27, THE MESSAGE

WEDNESDAY · FEBRUARY 29

Jesus said, "If you want to save your own life, you will lose it; but if you lose your life for me and for the gospel, you will save it."

Mark 8:35, GNT

THURSDAY · MARCH 1

God said to Abraham, "I will be your God and your children's God after you."

Genesis 17:7, CEB

FRIDAY · MARCH 2

If it is those who live by the Law who will gain the inheritance, faith is worthless and the promise is without force.

Romans 4:14, NJB

SATURDAY · MARCH 3

From you comes my praise in the great congregation;
   my vows I will pay before those who fear [the LORD].

Psalm 22:25, NRSV

Obedience is a listening process that empowers us to use our authority in a way that seems to be in tune with the will of God here and now.

DAVID A. FLEMING

SUNDAY · MARCH 4

SECOND SUNDAY IN LENT

Because of our sins [Jesus] was given over to die, and he was raised to life in order to put us right with God.

Romans 4:25, GNT

GENESIS 17:1-7, 15-16 · PSALM 22:23-31
ROMANS 4:13-25 · MARK 8:31-38

MONDAY · MARCH 5

Jesus said to the Jewish authorities, "Destroy this temple, and in three days I will raise it up."

John 2:19, NLT

TUESDAY · MARCH 6

God spoke these words, "Honor your father and your mother, so that your days may be long in the land that the LORD your God is giving you."

Exodus 20:12, NRSV

WEDNESDAY · MARCH 7

The heavens declare the glory of God;
the skies proclaim the work of his
hands.

Psalm 19:1, NIV

THURSDAY · MARCH 8

God spoke these words, "You shall not kill.
You shall not commit adultery. You
shall not steal. You shall not give false
evience against your neighbor."

Exodus 20:13-16, NJB

FRIDAY · MARCH 9

The Message that points to Christ on the Cross seems like sheer silliness to those hellbent on destruction, but for those on the way of salvation it makes perfect sense.

1 Corinthians 1:18, THE MESSAGE

SATURDAY · MARCH 10

The foolishness of God is wiser than human wisdom, and the weakness of God is stronger than human strength.

1 Corinthians 1:25, CEB

Prayer for Saint Patrick's Day:
I close my eyes to attractions. I close my ears to distractions. I close my heart to temptations. Calm me, O Lord, as you stilled the storm. Still me, O Lord; keep me from harm. Let all tumult within me cease.
Enfold me, Lord, in your peace.

GAELIC PRAYER

SUNDAY · MARCH 11

THIRD SUNDAY IN LENT

May the words of my mouth and the
  meditation of my heart
be pleasing in your sight,
O Lord, my Rock and my
  Redeemer.

Psalm 19:14, NIV

EXODUS 20:1-17 · PSALM 19
1 CORINTHIANS 1:18-25 · JOHN 2:13-22

MONDAY · MARCH 12

[The Israelites] complained [to God and Moses], "Why did you bring us out of Egypt to die in this desert, where there is no food or water? We can't stand any more of this miserable food!"

Numbers 21:5, GNT

TUESDAY · MARCH 13

God, being rich in faithful love, through the great love with which he loved us, even when we were dead in our sins, brought us to life with Christ.

Ephesians 2:4-5, NJB

WEDNESDAY · MARCH 14

Oh, thank GOD—he's so good!
His love never runs out.
All of you set free by GOD, tell the
world!

Psalm 107:1-2, THE MESSAGE

THURSDAY · MARCH 15

Jesus said, "God so loved the world, that he gave his only begotten Son, that whosoever believeth in him should not perish, but have everlasting life."

John 3:16, KJV

FRIDAY · MARCH 16

Jesus said, "God sent his Son into the world not to judge the world, but to save the world through him."
John 3:17, NLT

SATURDAY · MARCH 17

You are saved by God's grace because of your faith. This salvation is God's gift. It's not something you possessed.
Ephesians 2:8, CEB

The desert in our lives is the place where in our poverty, our sin and our need we come to know the Lord.

MARIA BOULDING

SUNDAY · MARCH 18

FOURTH SUNDAY IN LENT

Thank GOD for his marvelous love,
for his miracle mercy to the
children he loves.

Psalm 107:21, THE MESSAGE

NUMBERS 21:4-9 · PSALM 107:1-3, 17-22
EPHESIANS 2:1-10 · JOHN 3:14-21

MONDAY · MARCH 19

The Lord says, "The new covenant that I will make with the people of Israel will be this: I will put my law within them and write it on their hearts."

Jeremiah 31:33, GNT

TUESDAY · MARCH 20

Jesus said, "I assure you that unless a grain of wheat falls into the earth and dies, it can only be a single seed. But if it dies, it bears much fruit."

John 12:24, CEB

WEDNESDAY · MARCH 21

Jesus said, "When I am lifted up from the earth, I shall draw all people to myself."
John 12:32, NJB

THURSDAY · MARCH 22

I know my transgressions [O God],
and my sin is always before me.
Against you, you only, have I sinned
and done what is evil in your sight.
Psalm 51:3-4, NIV

FRIDAY · MARCH 23

Having been made perfect, [Jesus] became the source of eternal salvation for all who obey him.

Hebrews 5:9, NRSV

SATURDAY · MARCH 24

Christ did not honor himself by assuming he could become High Priest. No, he was chosen by God, who said to him, "You are my Son. Today I have become your Father."

Hebrews 5:5, NLT

Fasting is not meant to drag us down, but to still us. It is not meant to distract us from the really real, but rather to silence us so that we can hear things as they most truly are.

LAUREN WINNER

SUNDAY · MARCH 25

FIFTH SUNDAY IN LENT

Create a pure heart in me, O God,
   and put a new and loyal spirit in me.

Psalm 51:10, GNT

JEREMIAH 31:31-34 · PSALM 51:1-12
HEBREWS 5:5-10 · JOHN 12:20-33

MONDAY · MARCH 26

This is the day which the LORD hath made; we will rejoice and be glad in it.

Psalm 118:24, KJV

TUESDAY · MARCH 27

[Christ Jesus] made himself nothing, taking the very nature of a servant.

Philippians 2:7, NIV

WEDNESDAY · MARCH 28

With branches in your hands, start the festival
and march around the altar.

Psalm 118:27, GNT

THURSDAY · MARCH 29

The Sovereign LORD has given me his words of wisdom,
so that I know how to comfort the weary.

Isaiah 50:4, NLT

FRIDAY · MARCH 30

Let your face shine upon your servant
[O Lord];
save me in your steadfast love.
Psalm 31:16, NRSV

SATURDAY · MARCH 31

Thank God because he's good,
because his love never quits.
Psalm 118:1, THE MESSAGE

To love God with one's whole heart means to say a wholehearted yes to life and all that life brings with it. . . . To have the attitude that Jesus had when he said, "Not my will, but yours be done."

ANTHONY DE MELLO

SUNDAY · APRIL 1

PASSION/PALM SUNDAY

The people gave [Jesus] a wonderful welcome, some throwing their coats on the street, others spreading out rushes they had cut in the fields. . . . They were calling out, Hosanna! Blessed is he who comes in God's name!

Mark 11:8-9, THE MESSAGE

LITURGY OF THE PALMS: MARK 11:1-11 · PSALM 118:1-2, 19-29
LITURGY OF THE PASSION: ISAIAH 50:4-9a
PSALM 31:9-16 · PHILIPPIANS 2:5-11
MARK 14:1-15:47 OR MARK 15:1-39 (40-47)

MONDAY · APRIL 2

The LORD says,
"Here is my servant, whom I
 strengthen—
the one I have chosen, with whom I
 am pleased."

Isaiah 42:1, GNT

TUESDAY · APRIL 3

My life is an example to many,
 because you [O LORD] have been my
 strength and protection.
That is why I can never stop praising
 you.

Psalm 71:7-8, NLT

WEDNESDAY · APRIL 4

Think of the way [Jesus] persevered against such opposition from sinners and then you will not lose heart and come to grief.

Hebrews 12:3, NJB

THURSDAY · APRIL 5

MAUNDY THURSDAY

Jesus said, "If I, your Lord and teacher, have washed your feet, you too must wash each other's feet."

John 13:14, CEB

FRIDAY · APRIL 6

GOOD FRIDAY

When Jesus had received the wine, he said, "It is finished." Then he bowed his head and gave up his spirit.

John 19:30, NRSV

SATURDAY · APRIL 7

HOLY SATURDAY/EASTER VIGIL

This is what the Sovereign LORD says to these bones: I will make breath enter you, and you will come to life.

Ezekiel 37:5, NIV

Christ has turned all our sunsets into dawns.

CLEMENT OF ALEXANDRIA

SUNDAY · APRIL 8

EASTER DAY

The angel said, "Don't be alarmed! You are looking for Jesus of Nazareth, who was crucified. He has been raised. He isn't here. Look, here's the place where they laid him."

Mark 16:6. CEB

ACTS 10:34-43 · PSALM 118:1-2, 14-24
1 CORINTHIANS 15:1-11 · JOHN 20:1-18 OR MARK 16:1-8

MONDAY · APRIL 9

Jesus said, "Peace be with you," and, after saying this, he showed them his hands and his side. The disciples were filled with joy at seeing the Lord, and he said to them again, "Peace be with you."

John 20:20-21, NJB

TUESDAY · APRIL 10

Thomas said, "Unless I see the mark of the nails in his hands, and put my finger in the mark of the nails and my hand in his side, I will not believe."

John 20:25, NRSV

WEDNESDAY · APRIL 11

> How wonderful it is, how pleasant,
> for God's people to live together in
> harmony!
>
> Psalm 133:1, GNT

THURSDAY · APRIL 12

> The apostles testified powerfully to
> the resurrection of the Lord Jesus, and
> God's great blessing was upon them all.
>
> Acts 4:33, NLT

FRIDAY · APRIL 13

This, in essence, is the message we heard from Christ and are passing on to you: God is light, pure light; there's not a trace of darkness in him.

1 John 1:5, THE MESSAGE

SATURDAY · APRIL 14

[Jesus Christ] is the atoning sacrifice for our sins, and not only for ours but also for the sins of the whole world.

1 John 2:2, NIV

It is no mistake, I believe, that Mary Magdalene first looked at the risen Jesus . . . and saw, of all things, a gardener. Our task is not about death, the empty tomb, and the empty shroud. It is about planting, sowing and caring for hope in whatever garden we find ourselves.

MARY LOU KOWNACKI

SUNDAY · APRIL 15

> Jesus replied [to Thomas], "Do you believe because you see me? Happy are those who don't see and yet believe."
>
> John 20:29, CEB

ACTS 4:32-35 · PSALM 133
1 JOHN 1:1-2:2 · JOHN 20:19-31
OR MATTHEW 28:1-10

MONDAY · APRIL 16

Answer me when I call to you,
  O my righteous God.
Give me relief from my distress;
  be merciful to me and hear my
    prayer.

Psalm 4:1, NIV

TUESDAY · APRIL 17

See what love the Father has given us, that we should be called children of God; and that is what we are.

1 John 3:1, NRSV

WEDNESDAY · APRIL 18

Peter said, "Through faith in the name of Jesus, this man was healed—and you know how crippled he was before. Faith in Jesus' name has healed him before your very eyes."

Acts 3:16, NLT

THURSDAY · APRIL 19

Jesus said, "Everything written about me in the Law of Moses, the writings of the prophets, and the Psalms had to come true."

Luke 24:44, GNT

FRIDAY · APRIL 20

Children, do not let anyone lead you astray. Whoever acts uprightly is upright, just as [Christ] is upright.

1 John 3:7, NJB

SATURDAY · APRIL 21

Peter said, "Now it's time to change your ways! Turn to face God so he can wipe away your sins."

Acts 3:19, THE MESSAGE

When we begin to live a spirituality of simplicity, our primary concern ceases to be success and becomes faithfulness. We are called to live with integrity, to express the truth as we perceive it, and to trust in God's ability to use what we offer.

ELIZABETH J. CANHAM

SUNDAY · APRIL 22

What we know is that when Christ is openly revealed, we'll see him—and in seeing him, become like him.

1 John 3:2, THE MESSAGE

ACTS 3:12-19 · PSALM 4
1 JOHN 3:1-7 · LUKE 24:36b-48

MONDAY · APRIL 23

[The LORD] renews my strength.
He guides me along right paths,
  bringing honor to his name.

Psalm 23:3, NLT

TUESDAY · APRIL 24

Jesus said, "I am the good shepherd. The good shepherd lays down his life for the sheep."

John 10:11, NIV

WEDNESDAY · APRIL 25

Jesus said, "I am the good shepherd; I know my sheep and my sheep know me—just as the Father knows me and I know the Father."

John 10:14-15, NIV

THURSDAY · APRIL 26

Peter said, "Jesus is the stone you builders rejected; he has become the cornerstone!"

Acts 4:11, CEB

FRIDAY · APRIL 27

This is [God's] commandment, that we should believe in the name of his Son Jesus Christ and love one another, just as he has commanded us. All who obey his commandments abide in him, and he abides in them.

1 John 3:23-24, NRSV

SATURDAY · APRIL 28

Peter said, "Salvation is to be found through [Jesus Christ] alone; in all the world there is no one else whom God has given who can save us."

Acts 4:12, GNT

When we visit the sick, the elderly and the infirm, as he did, God is in our midst. And God is there at our table when we invoke Christ's name and enjoy the fruits of the earth.

MICHAEL DOWNEY

SUNDAY · APRIL 29

Surely goodness and mercy shall follow me all the days of my life: and I will dwell in the house of the Lord for ever.

Psalm 23:6, KJV

ACTS 4:5-12 · PSALM 23
1 JOHN 3:16-24 · JOHN 10:11-18

MONDAY · APRIL 30

The poor will eat as much as they want;
those who come to the Lord will
praise him.
May they prosper forever!
Psalm 22:26, GNT

TUESDAY · MAY 1

Jesus said, "I am the vine, you are the branches. Those who abide in me and I in them bear much fruit, because apart from me you can do nothing."
John 15:5, NRSV

WEDNESDAY · MAY 2

Whoever does not love does not know God, because God is love.

1 John 4:8, NIV

THURSDAY · MAY 3

Royal power belongs to the LORD. He rules all the nations.

Psalm 22:28, NLT

FRIDAY · MAY 4

Jesus said, "Live in me. Make your home in me just as I do in you."
John 15:4, THE MESSAGE

SATURDAY · MAY 5

Jesus said, "My Father is glorified when you produce much fruit and in this way prove that you are my disciples."
John 15:8, CEB

We must not grow weary of doing little things for the love of God, who looks not on the great size of the work, but on the love in it.

BROTHER LAWRENCE

SUNDAY · MAY 6

Dear friends, let us love one another, for love comes from God. Everyone who loves has been born of God and knows God.

1 John 4:7, NIV

ACTS 8:26-40 · PSALM 22:25-31
1 JOHN 4:7-21 · JOHN 15:1-8

MONDAY · MAY 7

> Shout your praises to GOD, everybody!
> Let loose and sing! Strike up the band!
> Psalm 98:4, THE MESSAGE

TUESDAY · MAY 8

> Our love for God means that we obey his commands.
> 1 John 5:3, GNT

WEDNESDAY · MAY 9

Jesus said, "When you obey my commandments, you remain in my love, just as I obey my Father's commandments and remain in his love."

John 15:10, NLT

THURSDAY · MAY 10

All the ends of the earth have seen the victory of our God.

Psalm 98:3, NRSV

FRIDAY · MAY 11

Jesus said, "My commandment is this: love one another, just as I love you. The greatest love you can have for your friends is to give your life for them."
John 15:12-13, GNT

SATURDAY · MAY 12

Who defeats the world? Isn't it the one who believes that Jesus is God's Son?
1 John 5:5, CEB

Perhaps in God's hands, the worst thing that happens to me can be transformed into the best thing that ever happened to me.

GRACE IMATHIU

SUNDAY · MAY 13

Jesus said, "You did not choose me, no, I chose you; and I commissioned you to go out and to bear fruit, fruit that will last."

John 15:16, NJB

ACTS 10:44-48 · PSALM 98
1 JOHN 5:1-6 · JOHN 15:9-17

MONDAY · MAY 14

Happy are those
   who reject the advice of evil people,
   who do not . . . join those who have
     no use for God.
Instead, they find joy in obeying the
   Law of the LORD.

Psalm 1:1-2, GNT

TUESDAY · MAY 15

This is the testimony: God gave us eternal life, and this life is in his Son.

1 John 5:11, NRSV

WEDNESDAY · MAY 16

They cast lots, and the lot fell to Matthias; so he was added to the eleven apostles.

Acts 1:26, NIV

THURSDAY · MAY 17

Jesus said, "Now I'm returning to you. I'm saying these things in the world's hearing so my people can experience my joy completed in them."

John 17:13, THE MESSAGE

FRIDAY · MAY 18

Jesus prayed, "I have revealed you to the ones you gave me from this world. They were always yours. You gave them to me, and they have kept your word."

John 17:6, NLT

SATURDAY · MAY 19

Jesus prayed, "Holy Father, watch over them in your name, the name you gave me, that they will be one just as we are one."

John 17:11, CEB

Hope is hearing the melody of the future. Faith is to dance to it now.

RUBEM ALVES

SUNDAY · MAY 20

Whoever has the Son, has life; whoever rejects the Son, rejects life.

1 John 5:12, THE MESSAGE

ACTS 1:15-17, 21-26 · PSALM 1
1 JOHN 5:9-13 · JOHN 17:6-19

MONDAY · MAY 21

> LORD, you have made so many things!
> How wisely you made them all!
>
> Psalm 104:24, GNT

TUESDAY · MAY 22

> Everyone who calls on the name of the Lord shall be saved.
>
> Acts 2:21, NRSV

WEDNESDAY · MAY 23

The Spirit too comes to help us in our weakness, for, when we do not know how to pray properly, then the Spirit personally makes our petitions for us in groans that cannot be put into words.

Romans 8:26, NJB

THURSDAY · MAY 24

Jesus said, "I tell you the truth: It is for your good that I am going away. Unless I go away, the Counselor will not come to you."

John 16:7, NIV

FRIDAY · MAY 25

Jesus said, "When the Spirit of the Truth comes, he will guide you in all truth."
John 16:13, CEB

SATURDAY · MAY 26

May all my thoughts be pleasing to him, for I rejoice in the LORD.
Psalm 104:34, NLT

The gift [of discernment] itself flows from a Source that far transcends our limited capacities. We may at points meet this Source as a subtle whispering of the Spirit within us. We may come to know it as the Holy Spirit working openly and boldly in our lives. We may encounter it in the risen Christ, present to teach and lead us along the way.

STEPHEN V. DOUGHTY WITH MARJORIE J. THOMPSON

SUNDAY · MAY 27

DAY OF PENTECOST

On the day of Pentecost all the believers were meeting together in one place.... Everyone present was filled with the Holy Spirit and began speaking in other languages, as the Holy Spirit gave them this ability.

Acts 2:1, 4, NLT

ACTS 2:1-21 · PSALM 104:24-34, 35b
ROMANS 8:22-27 · JOHN 15:26-27; 16:4b-15

MONDAY · MAY 28

Isaiah wrote, "Then I heard the Lord say, 'Whom shall I send? Who will be our messenger?'
    I answered, 'I will go! Send me!'"
Isaiah 6:8, GNT

TUESDAY · MAY 29

[God's Spirit] joins with our spirit to bear witness that we are children of God.
Romans 8:16, NJB

WEDNESDAY · MAY 30

This resurrection life you received from God is not a timid, grave-tending life. It's adventurously expectant.

Romans 8:15, THE MESSAGE

THURSDAY · MAY 31

The LORD will give strength unto his people; the LORD will bless his people with peace.

Psalm 29:11, KJV

FRIDAY · JUNE 1

Jesus said, "I assure you, unless someone is born anew, it's not possible to see God's kingdom."
John 3:3, CEB

SATURDAY · JUNE 2

Praise the LORD, you heavenly beings;
　praise his glory and power.
Praise the LORD's glorious name;
　bow down before the Holy One
　　when he appears.
Psalm 29:1-2, GNT

What happens when we enter into the silence of solitary prayer? We begin to let go of ourselves, which allows us to hear God. God is very gracious and patient. God does not usually interrupt us or push rudely into our affairs. If we choose to ignore God, God allows that. Such is the humility of a God who died on a cross.

DANIEL WOLPERT

SUNDAY · JUNE 3

TRINITY SUNDAY

Jesus said, "God so loved the world, that he gave his only begotten Son, that whosoever believeth in him should not perish, but have everlasting life."

John 3:16, KJV

ISAIAH 6:1-8 · PSALM 29
ROMANS 8:12-17 · JOHN 3:1-17

MONDAY · JUNE 4

Even though our physical being is gradually decaying, yet our spiritual being is renewed day after day.

2 Corinthians 4:16, GNT

TUESDAY · JUNE 5

GOD, high above, sees far below;
 no matter the distance, he knows
 everything about us.

Psalm 138:6, THE MESSAGE

WEDNESDAY · JUNE 6

Jesus said, "If a kingdom is divided against itself, that kingdom cannot stand. If a house is divided against itself, that house cannot stand."

Mark 3:24-25, NIV

THURSDAY · JUNE 7

We know that if the earthly tent we live in is destroyed, we have a building from God, a house not made with hands, eternal in the heavens.

2 Corinthians 5:1, NRSV

FRIDAY · JUNE 8

On the day I called [O LORD], you
answered me,
you increased my strength of soul.
Psalm 138:3, NRSV

SATURDAY · JUNE 9

Jesus said, "Whoever does God's will is
my brother, sister, and mother."
Mark 3:35, CEB

The divine call is not simply to do something great but to live close to God, to share God's loving intentions for the world.

MARJORIE J. THOMPSON AND STEPHEN D. BRYANT

SUNDAY · JUNE 10

> The LORD will work out his plans for
> my life—
> for your faithful love, O LORD,
> endures forever.
>
> Psalm 138:8, NLT

1 SAMUEL 8:4-20 (11:14-15) · PSALM 138
2 CORINTHIANS 4:13-5:1 · MARK 3:20-35

MONDAY · JUNE 11

The LORD said to Samuel, "I will show you what to do. You are to anoint for me the one I indicate."

1 Samuel 16:3, NIV

TUESDAY · JUNE 12

God does not see as human beings see; they look at appearances but [the LORD] looks at the heart.

1 Samuel 16:7, NJB

WEDNESDAY · JUNE 13

Samuel took the horn of oil, and anointed [David] in the presence of his brothers; and the spirit of the LORD came mightily upon David from that day forward.

1 Samuel 16:13, NRSV

THURSDAY · JUNE 14

Anyone who is joined to Christ is a new being; the old is gone, the new has come.

2 Corinthians 5:17, GNT

FRIDAY · JUNE 15

Paul wrote, "[Christ's] love has the first and last word in everything we do."
2 Corinthians 5:14, THE MESSAGE

SATURDAY · JUNE 16

Some nations boast of their chariots
and horses,
but we boast in the name of the
LORD our God.
Psalm 20:7, NLT

*The storm may rage,
but I am unshaken,
though the winds blow,
they leave me unmoved;
for the rock of my foundation
stands firm.*

PETER ABELARD

SUNDAY · JUNE 17

> What a beautiful thing, GOD, to give
>   thanks,
> to sing an anthem to you,
>   the High God!
>
> Psalm 92:1, THE MESSAGE

1 SAMUEL 15:34–16:13 · PSALM 20 OR PSALM 92
2 CORINTHIANS 5:6-10 (11-13), 14-17 · MARK 4:26-34

MONDAY · JUNE 18

Listen! This is the hour to receive God's favor; today is the day to be saved!

2 Corinthians 6:2, GNT

TUESDAY · JUNE 19

[Jesus] said to the lake, "Silence! Be still!" The wind settled down and there was a great calm.

Mark 4:39, CEB

WEDNESDAY · JUNE 20

[The disciples] were filled with great awe and said to one another, "Who then is this, that even the wind and the sea obey him?"
Mark 4:41, NRSV

THURSDAY · JUNE 21

The LORD is a shelter for the oppressed,
a refuge in times of trouble.
Psalm 9:9, NLT

FRIDAY · JUNE 22

David said to Saul, "The LORD who delivered me from the paw of the lion and the paw of the bear will deliver me from the hand of [Goliath]."

1 Samuel 17:37, NIV

SATURDAY · JUNE 23

[David] took his stick in his hand, selected five smooth stones from the river bed and put them in his shepherd's bag, in his pouch; then, sling in hand, he walked towards the Philistine [Goliath].

1 Samuel 17:40, NJB

As a fish swims the length and breadth of the sea and rests in its depths, as a bird flies through the air, so the Soul feels her mind completely unrestrained in the height, width, and depth of Love.

BEATRICE OF NAZARETH

SUNDAY · JUNE 24

David said to Goliath, "The whole world will know that there is a God in Israel. All those gathered here will know that it is not by sword or spear that the LORD saves."

1 Samuel 17:46-47, NIV

1 SAMUEL 17:(1a, 4-11, 19-23), 32-49 · PSALM 9:9-20
2 CORINTHIANS 6:1-13 · MARK 4:35-41

MONDAY · JUNE 25

Out of the depths I cry to you,
 O LORD;
O Lord, hear my voice.

Psalm 130:1-2, NIV

TUESDAY · JUNE 26

You are familiar with the generosity of our Master, Jesus Christ. Rich as he was, he gave it all away for us—in one stroke he became poor and we became rich.

2 Corinthians 8:9, THE MESSAGE

WEDNESDAY · JUNE 27

If you [O LORD] kept a record of our
  sins,
who could escape being condemned?
But you forgive us,
  so that we should stand in awe of
  you.

Psalm 130:3-4, GNT

THURSDAY · JUNE 28

[The sick woman] had heard about Jesus, and came up behind him in the crowd and touched his cloak, for she said, "If I but touch his clothes, I will be made well."

Mark 5:27-28, NRSV

FRIDAY · JUNE 29

[Jesus] said to her, "Daughter, your faith has made you well. Go in peace. Your suffering is over."

Mark 5:34, NLT

SATURDAY · JUNE 30

If you are eager to give, God will accept your gift on the basis of what you have to give, not on what you don't have.

2 Corinthians 8:12, GNT

Oh! If only we knew how much we need the grace and help of God, we would never lose sight of God, not even for a moment.

BROTHER LAWRENCE

SUNDAY · JULY 1

> O Israel, wait and watch for GOD—
> with GOD's arrival comes love,
> with GOD's arrival comes generous
> redemption.
>
> Psalm 130:7, THE MESSAGE

2 SAMUEL 1:1, 17-27 · PSALM 130
2 CORINTHIANS 8:7-15 · MARK 5:21-43

MONDAY · JULY 2

[David] grew stronger all the time, because the LORD God Almighty was with him.

2 Samuel 5:10, GNT

TUESDAY · JULY 3

The Lord said to Paul, "My grace is enough for you, because power is made perfect in weakness."

2 Corinthians 12:9, CEB

WEDNESDAY · JULY 4

Paul said, "I will boast all the more gladly of my weaknesses, so that the power of Christ may dwell in me."

2 Corinthians 12:9, NRSV

THURSDAY · JULY 5

Jesus said, "A prophet is honored everywhere except in his own hometown and among his relatives and his own family."

Mark 6:4, NLT

FRIDAY · JULY 6

[Jesus] summoned the Twelve and began to send them out in pairs, giving them authority over unclean spirits.

Mark 6:7, NJB

SATURDAY · JULY 7

[The Twelve] went out and preached that people should repent. They drove out many demons and anointed many sick people with oil and healed them.

Mark 6:12-13, NIV

As the soul goes ever after God with love so true, imbued with the spirit of suffering for His sake, God's majesty often and regularly grants it joy, and visits it sweetly and delectably in the Spirit; for the boundless love of Christ, the Word, cannot see the afflictions of his lover without comforting him or her.

JOHN OF THE CROSS

SUNDAY · JULY 8

> Within your Temple, O God,
> we meditate on your unfailing love.
>
> Psalm 48:9, NIV

2 SAMUEL 5:1-5, 9-10 · PSALM 48
2 CORINTHIANS 12:2-10 · MARK 6:1-13

MONDAY · JULY 9

The earth is the LORD's and all that is
in it
the world, and those who live in it.

Psalm 24:1, NRSV

TUESDAY · JULY 10

[God] chose us in Christ before the world was made to be holy and faultless before him in love.

Ephesians 1:4, NJB

WEDNESDAY · JULY 11

It's in Christ that we find out who we are and what we are living for.

Ephesians 1:11, THE MESSAGE

THURSDAY · JULY 12

God put his stamp of ownership on you by giving you the Holy Spirit he had promised.

Ephesians 1:13, GNT

FRIDAY · JULY 13

The Holy Spirit is the down payment on our inheritance, which is applied toward our redemption as God's own people, resulting in the honor of God's glory.
Ephesians 1:14, CEB

SATURDAY · JULY 14

Who may climb the mountain of the LORD?
  Who may stand in his holy place?
Only those whose hands and hearts are pure.
Psalm 24:3-4, NLT

Take from me, gracious God, all that separates me from you — my sense of past sin, my pride in present achievements, my anxieties for the future. Make me self-forgetful as I gaze on you, and let me know the joy of finding my true self in you. Amen.

HELEN JULIAN CSF

© REV. BROTHERJOHN GAUDREAU OEF. ALL RIGHTS RESERVED.

SUNDAY · JULY 15

In [Christ] we have redemption through his blood, the forgiveness of our trespasses, according to the riches of his grace.

Ephesians 1:7, NRSV

2 SAMUEL 6:1-5, 12b-19 · PSALM 24
EPHESIANS 1:3-14 · MARK 6:14-29

MONDAY · JULY 16

Jesus said to the apostles, "Come away to some lonely place all by yourselves and rest for a while."

Mark 6:31, NJB

TUESDAY · JULY 17

But now in Christ Jesus you who once were far away have been brought near through the blood of Christ.

Ephesians 2:13, NIV

WEDNESDAY · JULY 18

You [Gentiles] are no longer strangers and aliens. Rather, you are fellow citizens with God's people, and you belong to God's household.

Ephesians 2:19, CEB

THURSDAY · JULY 19

Wherever [Jesus] went . . . [people] brought their sick to the marketplace and begged him to let them touch the edge of his coat—that's all. And whoever touched him became well.

Mark 6:56, THE MESSAGE

FRIDAY · JULY 20

Christ himself has brought peace to us.
Ephesians 2:14, NLT

SATURDAY · JULY 21

God said, "I will not stop loving David
or fail to keep my promise to him."
Psalm 89:33, GNT

Without food, [people] can live but most a few weeks; without it, all other components of social justice are meaningless.

NORMAN BORLAUG

SUNDAY · JULY 22

All of us can come to the Father through the same Holy Spirit because of what Christ has done for us.

Ephesians 2:18, NLT

2 SAMUEL 7:1-14a · PSALM 89:20-37
EPHESIANS 2:11-22 · MARK 6:30-34, 53-56

MONDAY · JULY 23

Jesus took the loaves, and when he had given thanks, he distributed them to those who were seated; so also the fish, as much as they wanted.

John 6:11, NRSV

TUESDAY · JULY 24

When [the crowd] had plenty to eat, [Jesus] said to his disciples, "Gather up the leftover pieces, so that nothing will be wasted."

John 6:12, CEB

WEDNESDAY · JULY 25

The people realized that God was at work among them in what Jesus had just done.

John 6:14, THE MESSAGE

THURSDAY · JULY 26

You may mock the plans of the poor, but [the LORD] is their refuge.

Psalm 14:6, NJB

FRIDAY · JULY 27

Paul wrote, "I pray that Christ will make his home in your hearts through faith. I pray that you may have your roots and foundation in love."

Ephesians 3:17, GNT

SATURDAY · JULY 28

Oh, that salvation for Israel would
  come out of Zion!
When the LORD restores the
  fortunes of his people,
let Jacob rejoice and Israel be glad!

Psalm 14:7, NIV

Prayer draws us into unity with Christ, into communion and community. Compassionate action results, growing out of the love of God. We receive the love of God and return that love in grateful devotion. We pray, not to get what we want from God but to consent to what God wants. Prayer expresses relationship, sometimes with words, sometimes deeper than words can express.

J. DAVID MUYSKENS

SUNDAY · JULY 29

May you experience the love of Christ, though it is too great to understand fully. Then you will be made complete with all the fullness of life and power that comes from God.

Ephesians 3:19, NLT

2 SAMUEL 11:1-15 · PSALM 14
EPHESIANS 3:14-21 · JOHN 6:1-21

MONDAY · JULY 30

Jesus said, "What God wants you to do is to believe in the one he sent."

John 6:29, GNT

TUESDAY · JULY 31

You are one body and one spirit just as God also called you in one hope.

Ephesians 4:4, CEB

WEDNESDAY · AUGUST 1

Create in me a clean heart, O God; and renew a right spirit within me.

Psalm 51:10, KJV

THURSDAY · AUGUST 2

God wants us to grow up, to know the whole truth and tell it in love—like Christ in everything.

Ephesians 4:15, THE MESSAGE

FRIDAY · AUGUST 3

Restore to me the joy of your salvation
[O God],
and sustain in me a willing spirit.

Psalm 51:12, NRSV

SATURDAY · AUGUST 4

Now these are the gifts Christ gave to the church: the apostles, the prophets, the evangelists, and the pastors and teachers. Their responsibility is to equip God's people to do his work and build up the church, the body of Christ.

Ephesians 4:11-12, NLT

I am waiting, Lord, I am expecting, I am hoping. Do not leave me without your Spirit. Give me your unifying and consoling Spirit. Amen.

HENRI J. M. NOUWEN

SUNDAY · AUGUST 5

Jesus said, "I am the bread of life. Whoever comes to me will never be hungry, and whoever believes in me will never be thirsty."

John 6:35, NRSV

2 SAMUEL 11:26-12:13a · PSALM 51:1-12
EPHESIANS 4:1-16 · JOHN 6:24-35

MONDAY · AUGUST 6

> I wait for the LORD, my soul waits,
> and in his word I put my hope.
>
> Psalm 130:5, NIV

TUESDAY · AUGUST 7

> Even if you are angry, do not sin: never let the sun set on your anger.
>
> Ephesians 4:26, NJB

WEDNESDAY · AUGUST 8

Live a life filled with love, following the example of Christ.

Ephesians 5:2, NLT

THURSDAY · AUGUST 9

Jesus said, "I am the living bread that came down from heaven. If you eat this bread, you will live forever."

John 6:51, GNT

FRIDAY · AUGUST 10

Jesus said, "Don't grumble among yourselves. No one can come to me unless they are drawn to me by the Father who sent me."

John 6:43-44, CEB

SATURDAY · AUGUST 11

[God's] Holy Spirit, moving and breathing in you, is the most intimate part of your life, making you fit for himself. Don't take such a gift for granted.

Ephesians 4:30, THE MESSAGE

Therefore, if we wish to pray—and by this I mean open ourselves up to the possibility that God will speak to us, teach us, transform us—we must allow space in the busy world we have created. Like the ones who went into the desert, we must go to a place where the world does not overwhelm us.

DANIEL WOLPERT

SUNDAY · AUGUST 12

> Out of the depths I cry to you,
>   O LORD.
> O Lord, hear my voice.
>
> Psalm 130:1-2, NIV

2 SAMUEL 18:5-9, 15, 31-33 · PSALM 130
EPHESIANS 4:25–5:2 · JOHN 6:35, 41-51

MONDAY · AUGUST 13

Do not be foolish, but understand what the will of the Lord is.

Ephesians 5:17, NRSV

TUESDAY · AUGUST 14

Jesus said, "Those who eat my flesh and drink my blood have eternal life, and I will raise them to life on the last day."

John 6:54, GNT

WEDNESDAY · AUGUST 15

How amazing are the deeds of the
 LORD!
All who delight in him should
 ponder them.
Psalm 111:2, NLT

THURSDAY · AUGUST 16

All [the LORD] does is full of honor
 and majesty;
his righteousness is eternal.
Psalm 111:3, GNT

FRIDAY · AUGUST 17

The fear of the LORD is the beginning of wisdom.
Psalm 111:10, KJV

SATURDAY · AUGUST 18

Be filled with the Spirit in the following ways: speak to each other with psalms, hymns, and spiritual songs; sing and make music to the Lord in your hearts.
Ephesians 5:18-19, CEB

One of the greatest obstacles facing us on the road to spiritual formation is our lack of appreciation for our infinite worth in the eyes of God. No matter what faults and failings may hamper us on our way home to our Father's house, God loves and forgives and welcomes us.

MEETING GOD IN SCRIPTURE: ENTERING THE NEW TESTAMENT

© REV. BROTHERJOHN GAUDREAU OEF. ALL RIGHTS RESERVED.

SUNDAY · AUGUST 19

> Sing praises over everything, any excuse for a song to God the Father in the name of our Master, Jesus Christ.
>
> Ephesians 5:20, THE MESSAGE

MONDAY · AUGUST 20

Jesus said, "It is the spirit that gives life, the flesh has nothing to offer."

John 6:63, NJB

TUESDAY · AUGUST 21

Solomon prayed, "Give attention to your servant's prayer and his plea for mercy, O LORD my God. Hear the cry and the prayer that your servant is praying in your presence this day."

1 Kings 8:28, NIV

WEDNESDAY · AUGUST 22

Happy are those whose strength is in you [O God],
in whose heart are the highways to Zion.

Psalm 84:5, NRSV

THURSDAY · AUGUST 23

Truth, righteousness, peace, faith, and salvation are more than words. Learn how to apply them.

Ephesians 6:14, THE MESSAGE

FRIDAY · AUGUST 24

Pray in the Spirit at all times and on every occasion. Stay alert and be persistent in your prayers for all believers everywhere.

Ephesians 6:18, NLT

SATURDAY · AUGUST 25

One day spent in your Temple
 [O God]
 is better than a thousand anywhere else.

Psalm 84:10, GNT

The Cross compels us to become fully alive, not by avoiding pain and loss but by passing through them.

JOSEPH R. VENEROSO

SUNDAY · AUGUST 26

Peter said to Jesus, "We have come to believe and know that you are the Holy One of God."

John 6:69, NRSV

1 KINGS 8:(1, 6, 10-11), 22-30, 41-43 · PSALM 84
EPHESIANS 6:10-20 · JOHN 6:56-69

MONDAY · AUGUST 27

Don't just listen to God's word. You must do what it says. Otherwise, you are only fooling yourselves.

James 1:22, NLT

TUESDAY · AUGUST 28

[God] opens a place in his heart for the
    down-and-out,
he restores the wretched of the
    earth.

Psalm 72:13, THE MESSAGE

WEDNESDAY · AUGUST 29

Jesus said, "There is nothing that goes into you from the outside which can make you ritually unclean. Rather, it is what comes out of you that makes you unclean."

Mark 7:15, GNT

THURSDAY · AUGUST 30

Everyone should be quick to listen, slow to speak and slow to become angry.

James 1:19, NIV

FRIDAY · AUGUST 31

If those who claim devotion to God don't control what they say, they mislead themselves. Their devotion is worthless.

James 1:26, CEB

SATURDAY · SEPTEMBER 1

Jesus answered the Pharisees, "How rightly Isaiah prophesied . . . :
'This people honors me only with
    lip-service,
while their hearts are far from me.'"

Mark 7:6, NJB

Be happy in the moment, that's enough. Each moment is all we need, not more. Be happy now and if you show through your actions that you love others, including those who are poorer than you, you'll give them happiness, too. . . . So smile, be cheerful, be joyous that God loves you.

MOTHER TERESA

SUNDAY · SEPTEMBER 2

Every good and perfect gift is from above, coming down from the Father of the heavenly lights.

James 1:17, NIV

SONG OF SOLOMON 2:8-13 · PSALM 45:1-2, 6-9 OR PSALM 72
JAMES 1:17-27 · MARK 7:1-8, 14-15, 21-23

MONDAY · SEPTEMBER 3

The rich and the poor have this in common:
the LORD is the maker of them all.

Proverbs 22:2, NRSV

TUESDAY · SEPTEMBER 4

The people said of Jesus, "Everything he does is wonderful. He even makes the deaf to hear and gives speech to those who cannot speak."

Mark 7:37, NLT

WEDNESDAY · SEPTEMBER 5

You will be doing the right thing if you obey the law of the Kingdom, which is found in the scripture, "Love your neighbor as you love yourself."

James 2:8, GNT

THURSDAY · SEPTEMBER 6

Those who are generous are blessed, for they share their bread with the poor.

Proverbs 22:9, NRSV

FRIDAY · SEPTEMBER 7

Those who trust in the LORD are like Mount Zion,
which cannot be shaken but endures forever.

Psalm 125:1, NIV

SATURDAY · SEPTEMBER 8

My brothers and sisters, what good is it if people say they have faith but do nothing to show it? Claiming to have faith can't save anyone, can it?

James 2:14, CEB

We want God's voice to be clear, but it is not. . . . We want it to be clear as day, but it is deep as night. It is deep and clear, but with a dark clarity like an xray. It reaches our bones.

ERNESTO CARDENAL

SUNDAY · SEPTEMBER 9

> Faith by itself, if it is not accompanied by action, is dead.
>
> James 2:17, NIV

PROVERBS 22:1-2, 8-9, 22-23 · PSALM 125 OR PSALM 124
JAMES 2:1-10 (11-13) 14-17 · MARK 7:24-37

MONDAY · SEPTEMBER 10

Even though the tongue is a small part of the body, it boasts wildly.

James 3:5, CEB

TUESDAY · SEPTEMBER 11

[Jesus] asked his disciples, "Who do people say that I am?" And they answered him, "John the Baptist; and others, Elijah; and still others, one of the prophets."

Mark 8:27-28, NRSV

WEDNESDAY · SEPTEMBER 12

Jesus asked his disciples, "Who do you say I am?" Peter spoke up and said to him, "You are the Christ."

Mark 8:29, NJB

THURSDAY · SEPTEMBER 13

The law of the LORD is perfect;
  it gives new strength.
The commands of the LORD are
    trustworthy,
  giving wisdom to those who lack it.

Psalm 19:7, GNT

FRIDAY · SEPTEMBER 14

Calling the crowd to join his disciples, [Jesus] said, "If any of you wants to be my follower, you must turn from your selfish ways, take up your cross, and follow me."

Mark 8:34, NLT

SATURDAY · SEPTEMBER 15

With our tongues we bless God our Father; with the same tongues we curse the very men and women he made in his image.... My friends, this can't go on.

James 3:9-10, THE MESSAGE

For Jesus, how we treat others is at least as important as how we treat God.

CHRISTOPHER MARICLE

SUNDAY · SEPTEMBER 16

Let the words of my mouth, and the meditation of my heart, be acceptable in thy sight, O LORD, my strength, and my redeemer.

Psalm 19:14, KJV

PROVERBS 1:20-33 · PSALM 19
JAMES 3:1-12 · MARK 8:27-38

MONDAY · SEPTEMBER 17

Are there any of you who are wise and understanding? You are to prove it by your good life, by your good deeds performed with humility and wisdom.

James 3:13, GNT

TUESDAY · SEPTEMBER 18

Jesus said, "Whoever wants to be first must be last of all and servant of all."

Mark 9:35, NRSV

WEDNESDAY · SEPTEMBER 19

Jesus said, "Whoever welcomes one of these children in my name welcomes me; and whoever welcomes me isn't actually welcoming me but rather the one who sent me."

Mark 9:37, CEB

THURSDAY · SEPTEMBER 20

Oh, the joys of those who do not
 follow the advice of the wicked,
 or stand around with sinners,
 or join in with mockers.
But they delight in the law of the LORD.

Psalm 1:1-2, NLT

FRIDAY · SEPTEMBER 21

Jesus said, "The Son of Man is to be betrayed into human hands, and they will kill him, and three days after being killed, he will rise again."

Mark 9:31, NRSV

SATURDAY · SEPTEMBER 22

The woman to be admired and praised
is the woman who lives in the Fear-
of-God.
Give her everything she deserves!
Festoon her life with praises!

Proverbs 31:30-31, THE MESSAGE

Walk on always, in the name of God, although it may seem to you that you have neither strength nor courage to put one foot in front of the other. . . . If you abandon yourself to God, he will not fail to help your powerlessness.

FRANCOIS FÉNELON

SUNDAY · SEPTEMBER 23

> Come close to God, and God will come close to you.
>
> James 4:8, NLT

PROVERBS 31:10-31 · PSALM 1
JAMES 3:13–4:3, 7-8a · MARK 9:30-37

MONDAY · SEPTEMBER 24

Our help is in the name of the LORD,
the Maker of heaven and earth.
Psalm 124:8, NIV

TUESDAY · SEPTEMBER 25

Jesus said, "Have the salt of friendship among yourselves, and live in peace with one another."
Mark 9:50, GNT

WEDNESDAY · SEPTEMBER 26

My dear friends, if you know people who have wandered off from God's truth, don't write them off. Go after them.

James 5:19, THE MESSAGE

THURSDAY · SEPTEMBER 27

If any of you are suffering, they should pray. If any of you are happy, they should sing.

James 5:13, CEB

FRIDAY · SEPTEMBER 28

Are any among you sick? They should call for the elders of the church and have them pray over them, anointing them with oil in the name of the Lord.

James 5:14, NRSV

SATURDAY · SEPTEMBER 29

Jesus said, "Whoever isn't against us is for us."

Mark 9:40, CEB

No one is born hating another person because of the color of his skin, or his background, or his religion. People must learn to hate, and if they can learn to hate, they can be taught to love, for love comes more naturally to the human heart than its opposite.

NELSON MANDELA

© REV. BROTHERJOHN GAUDREAU OEF. ALL RIGHTS RESERVED.

SUNDAY · SEPTEMBER 30

Confess your sins to each other and pray for each other so that you may be healed. The prayer of the righteous person is powerful in what it can achieve.

James 5:16, CEB

ESTHER 7:1-6, 9-10; 9:20-22 · PSALM 124
JAMES 5:13-20 · MARK 9:38-50

MONDAY · OCTOBER 1

To you, O LORD, I lift up my soul;
in you I trust, O my God.

Psalm 25:1-2, NIV

TUESDAY · OCTOBER 2

Long ago God spoke to our ancestors in many and various ways by the prophets, but in these last days he has spoken to us by a Son.

Hebrews 1:1-2, NRSV

WEDNESDAY · OCTOBER 3

Job said, "When God sends us something good, we welcome it. How can we complain when he sends us trouble?"

Job 2:10, GNT

THURSDAY · OCTOBER 4

Jesus said to his disciples, "Don't push these children away. Don't ever get between them and me. These children are at the very center of life in the kingdom."

Mark 10:14, THE MESSAGE

FRIDAY · OCTOBER 5

Jesus and the ones he makes holy have the same Father. That is why Jesus is not ashamed to call them his brothers and sisters.

Hebrews 2:11, NLT

SATURDAY · OCTOBER 6

Direct me in your ways, [O LORD],
and teach me your paths.
Encourage me to walk in your truth.

Psalm 25:4-5, NJB

God's hospitality to us is linked to our hospitality to those who have little or nothing. If we avoid Christ in the poor, we are avoiding the gate to heaven.

JIM FOREST

SUNDAY · OCTOBER 7

WORLD COMMUNION SUNDAY

I love the house where you live,
   O LORD,
      the place where your glory dwells.

Psalm 26:8, NIV

JOB 1:1; 2:1-10 · PSALM 26 OR PSALM 25
HEBREWS 1:1-4; 2:5-12 · MARK 10:2-16

MONDAY · OCTOBER 8

My God, my God, why have you
abandoned me?
I have cried desperately for help,
but still it does not come.

Psalm 22:1, GNT

TUESDAY · OCTOBER 9

The word of God is living and
active, sharper than any two-edged
sword . . . ; it is able to judge the
thoughts and intentions of the heart.

Hebrews 4:12, NRSV

Wednesday · October 10

We do not have a high priest who is unable to sympathize with our weaknesses, but we have one who has been tempted in every way, just as we are—yet was without sin.

Hebrews 4:15, NIV

Thursday · October 11

Let us, then, have no fear in approaching the throne of grace to receive mercy and to find grace when we are in need of help.

Hebrews 4:16, NJB

FRIDAY · OCTOBER 12

Nothing in all creation is hidden from God.

Hebrews 4:13, NLT

SATURDAY · OCTOBER 13

Jesus said, "It's easier for a camel to squeeze through the eye of a needle than for a rich person to enter God's kingdom."

Mark 10:25, CEB

Our present ecological crisis . . . has, religious people would say, a great deal to do with our failure to think of the world as existing in relation to the mystery of God, not just as a huge warehouse of stuff to be used for our convenience.

ROWAN WILLIAMS

© REV. BROTHERJOHN GAUDREAU OEF. ALL RIGHTS RESERVED.

SUNDAY · OCTOBER 14

Jesus said, "All things are possible with God."
Mark 10:27, NIV

JOB 23:1-9, 16-17 · PSALM 22:1-15
HEBREWS 4:12-16 · MARK 10:17-31

MONDAY · OCTOBER 15

Jesus said, "Anyone who wants to become great among you must be your servant, and anyone who wants to be first among you must be slave to all."

Mark 10:43-44, NJB

TUESDAY · OCTOBER 16

O Lord, what a variety of things you have made!
In wisdom you have made them all.
The earth is full of your creatures.

Psalm 104:24, NLT

WEDNESDAY · OCTOBER 17

During his days on earth, Christ offered prayers and requests with loud cries and tears as his sacrifices to the one who was able to save him from death. He was heard because of his godly devotion.

Hebrews 5:7, CEB

THURSDAY · OCTOBER 18

Even though [Jesus] was God's Son, he learned through his sufferings to be obedient.

Hebrews 5:8, GNT

FRIDAY · OCTOBER 19

GOD *said to Job*,
"Why do you talk without knowing
 what you're talking about? . . .
Where were you when I created the
 earth?
Tell me, since you know so much!"
Job 38:2, 4, THE MESSAGE

SATURDAY · OCTOBER 20

Jesus said, "The Son of Man came not to be served but to serve."
Mark 10:45, NRSV

Dear Jesus, during this day help me quiet all the thoughts that fill my head—where I must go, whom I must see, and what I must do. In their place, give me a sense of your order, your peace, and your time. . . .

I give all my tasks to you and trust you to bring order to them. In these moments, dear Jesus, come to me, be with me, and free me from the tyranny of "to do."

PATRICIA F. WILSON

SUNDAY · OCTOBER 21

> O Lord, my God, how great you are!
> You are clothed with majesty and glory;
>   you cover yourself with light.
> You have spread out the heavens like
>   a tent
>   and built your home on the waters
>   above.
>
> Psalm 104:1-3, GNT

JOB 38:1-7 (34-41) • PSALM 104:1-9, 24, 35c
HEBREWS 5:1-10 • MARK 10:35-45

MONDAY · OCTOBER 22

[Jesus] holds the office of priest permanently because he continues to serve forever. This is why he can completely save those who are approaching God through him, because he always lives to speak with God for them.

Hebrews 7:24-25, CEB

TUESDAY · OCTOBER 23

We have a high priest who perfectly fits our needs: completely holy, uncompromised by sin, with authority extending as high as God's presence in heaven itself.

Hebrews 7:26, THE MESSAGE

WEDNESDAY · OCTOBER 24

After Job had prayed for his friends, the LORD made him prosperous again and gave him twice as much as he had before.

Job 42:10, NIV

THURSDAY · OCTOBER 25

I will bless the LORD at all times: his praise shall continually be in my mouth.

Psalm 34:1, KJV

FRIDAY · OCTOBER 26

> In my desperation I prayed, and the
> LORD listened;
> he saved me from all my troubles.
>
> Psalm 34:6, NLT

SATURDAY · OCTOBER 27

> Then Job answered the LORD:
> "I know that you can do all things,
> and that no purpose of yours can be
> thwarted."
>
> Job 42:1-2, NRSV

A saint is one who exaggerates what the world and the church have forgotten.

G. K. CHESTERTON

SUNDAY · OCTOBER 28

> When [the blind man, Bartimaeus] heard that Jesus the Nazarene was passing by, he began to cry out, "Son of David, Jesus! Mercy, have mercy on me!"
>
> Mark 10:47, THE MESSAGE

JOB 42:1-6, 10-17 · PSALM 34:1-8 (19-22)
HEBREWS 7:23-28 · MARK 10:46-52

MONDAY · OCTOBER 29

The voice from the throne said, "Look! God's dwelling is here with humankind. He will dwell with them, and they will be his peoples. God himself will be with them as their God."

Revelation 21:3, CEB

TUESDAY · OCTOBER 30

The world and all that is in it belong to
  the LORD;
The earth and all who live on it are
  his.

Psalm 24:1, GNT

WEDNESDAY · OCTOBER 31

[The one who was seated on the throne said], "It is done! I am the Alpha and the Omega, the beginning and the end."

Revelation 21:6, NRSV

THURSDAY · NOVEMBER 1

ALL SAINTS DAY

Jesus said [to Martha], "Did I not tell you that if you believed, you would see the glory of God?"

John 11:40, NIV

FRIDAY · NOVEMBER 2

> [The LORD] will swallow up death
>   forever!
> The Sovereign LORD will wipe away
>   all tears.
> He will remove forever all insults and
>   mockery
>   against his land and people.
> The LORD has spoken!
>
> Isaiah 25:8, NLT

SATURDAY · NOVEMBER 3

> On that day, it will be said,
> "Look, this is our God,
> in him we put our hope that he should
>   save us.
>
> Isaiah 25:9, NJB

The purpose of the Sabbath is to clear away the distractions of our lives so we can rest in God and experience God's grace in a new way.

LYNNE M. BABB

© REV. BROTHERJOHN GAUDREAU OEF. ALL RIGHTS RESERVED.

SUNDAY · NOVEMBER 4

[God] will wipe every tear from their eyes. There will be no more death or mourning or crying or pain, for the old order of things has passed away.

Revelation 21:4, NIV

RUTH 1:1-18 · PSALM 146
HEBREWS 9:11-14 · MARK 12:28-34

MONDAY · NOVEMBER 5

As a deer yearns
   for running streams,
so I yearn
   for you, my God.

Psalm 42:1, NJB

TUESDAY · NOVEMBER 6

Christ, having been offered once to bear the sins of many, will appear a second time, not to deal with sin, but to save those who are eagerly waiting for him.

Hebrews 9:28, NRSV

WEDNESDAY · NOVEMBER 7

Jesus said, "I assure you that this poor widow has put in more than everyone.... All of them are giving out of their spare change. But she from her hopeless poverty has given everything she had, even what she needed to live on."

Mark 12:43-44, CEB

THURSDAY · NOVEMBER 8

Jesus said, "Watch out for the religion scholars. They love to walk around in academic gowns, preening in the radiance of public flattery.... And all the time they are exploiting the weak and helpless."

Mark 12:38, 40, THE MESSAGE

FRIDAY · NOVEMBER 9

Unless the LORD builds a house,
the work of the builders is wasted.
Psalm 127:1, NLT

SATURDAY · NOVEMBER 10

May the LORD show his constant love
during the day,
so that I may have a song at night,
a prayer to the God of my life.
Psalm 42:8, GNT

This life is not all there is. More awaits us, and prayer makes it possible for us to catch a glimpse of eternal life. Prayer becomes a means of grace that enables us to loosen our hold on time so that we can put our hands on eternity.

STEVE HARPER

SUNDAY · NOVEMBER 11

> [Christ] has appeared once for all at the end of the age to remove sin by the sacrifice of himself.
>
> Hebrews 9:26, NRSV

RUTH 3:1-5; 4:13-17 · PSALM 127 OR PSALM 42
HEBREWS 9:24-28 · MARK 12:38-44

MONDAY · NOVEMBER 12

> No one is holy like the LORD;
> there is none like him,
> no protector like our God.
>
> 1 Samuel 2:2, GNT

TUESDAY · NOVEMBER 13

> Jesus said to [his disciples]: "Watch out that no one deceives you. Many will come in my name, claiming, 'I am he.'"
>
> Mark 13:5-6, NIV

WEDNESDAY · NOVEMBER 14

> [God] picks up the poor from out of
> the dirt,
> rescues the wretched who've been
> thrown out with the trash,
> Seats them among the honored guests.
>
> Psalm 113:7-8, THE MESSAGE

THURSDAY · NOVEMBER 15

> Let us hold tightly without wavering to the hope we affirm, for God can be trusted to keep his promise.
>
> Hebrews 10:23, NLT

FRIDAY · NOVEMBER 16

Let's also think about how to motivate each other to show love and to do good works.

Hebrews 10:24, CEB

SATURDAY · NOVEMBER 17

Do not absent yourself from your own assemblies, as some do, but encourage each other.

Hebrews 10:25, NJB

I do not at all understand the mystery of grace — only that it meets us where we are but does not leave us where it found us.

ANNE LAMOTT

© REV. BROTHERJOHN GAUDREAU OEF. ALL RIGHTS RESERVED.

SUNDAY · NOVEMBER 18

> From the rising of the sun to the place where it sets,
> the name of the LORD is to be praised.
>
> Psalm 113:3, NIV

1 SAMUEL 1:4-20 · 1 SAMUEL 2:1-10 OR PSALM 113
HEBREWS 10:11-14 (15-18) 19-25 · MARK 13:1-8

MONDAY · NOVEMBER 19

Jesus said, "I was born and came into the world to testify to the truth. All who love the truth recognize that what I say is true."

John 18:37, NLT

TUESDAY · NOVEMBER 20

Grace and peace to you from the one who is and was and is coming.

Revelation 1:4, CEB

WEDNESDAY · NOVEMBER 21

One who rules over people justly,
 ruling in the fear of God,
is like the light of morning...
 gleaming from the rain on the
 grassy land.

2 Samuel 23:3-4, NRSV

THURSDAY · NOVEMBER 22

THANKSGIVING DAY

King David said,
"I will allow no sleep to my eyes,
 no slumber to my eyelids,
till I find a place for the LORD."

Psalm 132:4-5, NIV

FRIDAY · NOVEMBER 23

Glory and strength to Christ, who loves us, who blood-washed our sins from our lives.

Revelation 1:5, THE MESSAGE

SATURDAY · NOVEMBER 24

To Jesus Christ be the glory and power forever and ever! Amen.

Revelation 1:6, GNT

Being in God's creation often slows us down, which enables us to notice beauty, which in turn creates thankfulness and an attitude of receptivity. Nature often helps us listen to God more easily, particularly when we let our minds drift a bit.

LYNNE M. BABB

© REV. BROTHERJOHN GAUDREAU OEF. ALL RIGHTS RESERVED.

SUNDAY · NOVEMBER 25

CHRIST THE KING/REIGN OF CHRIST

"Let us go to the LORD's house;
　　let us worship before his throne."

Psalm 132:7, GNT

2 SAMUEL 23:1-7 · PSALM 132:1-12 (13-18)
REVELATION 1:4b-8 · JOHN 18:33-37

MONDAY · NOVEMBER 26

Jesus said, "Pray constantly that you will have the strength and wits to make it through everything that's coming and end up on your feet before the Son of Man."

Luke 21:36, THE MESSAGE

TUESDAY · NOVEMBER 27

To you, O LORD, I lift up my soul;
in you I trust, O my God.

Psalm 25:1-2, NIV

WEDNESDAY · NOVEMBER 28

Show me your ways, O LORD,
 teach me your paths;
guide me in your truth and teach me.

Psalm 25:4-5, NIV

THURSDAY · NOVEMBER 29

May [the Lord] so strengthen your hearts in holiness that you may be blameless before our God and Father at the coming of our Lord Jesus with all his saints.

1 Thessalonians 3:13, NRSV

FRIDAY · NOVEMBER 30

Do not remember the rebellious sins of
my youth.
Remember me in the light of your
unfailing love,
for you are merciful, O LORD.
Psalm 25:7, NLT

SATURDAY · DECEMBER 1

Jesus said, "Heaven and earth shall pass away; but my words shall not pass away."
Luke 21:33, KJV

Who knows in what partial ways the long-expected one appears, in what disguise the coming one comes.

FREDERICK BUECHNER

SUNDAY · DECEMBER 2

FIRST SUNDAY OF ADVENT

May God our Father himself and our Master Jesus clear the road to you! And may the Master pour on the love so it fills your lives and splashes over on everyone around you.

1 Thessalonians 3:11-12, THE MESSAGE

JEREMIAH 33:14-16 · PSALM 25:1-10
1 THESSALONIANS 3:9-13 · LUKE 21:25-36

MONDAY · DECEMBER 3

John went throughout the whole territory of the Jordan River, preaching, "Turn away from your sins and be baptized, and God will forgive your sins."

Luke 3:3, GNT

TUESDAY · DECEMBER 4

As it is written in the book of the words of [Isaiah] the prophet, saying, The voice of one crying in the wilderness, Prepare ye the way of the Lord, make his paths straight.

Luke 3:4, KJV

WEDNESDAY · DECEMBER 5

The Lord Almighty says, "Look! I am sending my messenger, and he will prepare the way before me."
Malachi 3:1, NLT

THURSDAY · DECEMBER 6

Who can endure the day of [the Lord's] coming? Who can stand when he appears?
Malachi 3:2, NIV

FRIDAY · DECEMBER 7

Paul wrote to the Philippian Christians, "I thank my God every time I remember you, constantly praying with joy in every one of my prayers for all of you."
Philippians 1:3-4, NRSV

SATURDAY · DECEMBER 8

Paul wrote, "I'm sure about this: the one who started a good work in you will stay with you to complete the job by the day of Christ Jesus."
Philippians 1:6, CEB

O holy Child of Bethlehem, descend to us, we pray:
cast out our sin, and enter in, be born in us today.
We hear the Christmas angels the great glad tidings tell;
O come to us, abide with us, Our Lord Emmanuel.

PHILLIPS BROOKS

SUNDAY · DECEMBER 9

SECOND SUNDAY OF ADVENT

Zechariah proclaimed,
"Praise the Lord, the God of Israel,
because he has visited and redeemed
his people."

Luke 1:68, NLT

MALACHI 3:1-4 · LUKE 1:68-79
PHILIPPIANS 1:3-11 · LUKE 3:1-6

MONDAY · DECEMBER 10

As fresh water brings joy to the thirsty, so God's people rejoice when he saves them.

Isaiah 12:3, GNT

TUESDAY · DECEMBER 11

Never worry about anything; but tell God all your desires of every kind in prayer and petition shot through with gratitude.

Philippians 4:6, NJB

WEDNESDAY · DECEMBER 12

> The LORD your God is with you,
>   he is mighty to save.
> He will take great delight in you,
>   he will quiet you with his love.
>
> Zephaniah 3:17, NIV

THURSDAY · DECEMBER 13

> Rejoice in the Lord always.
>
> Philippians 4:4, NRSV

FRIDAY · DECEMBER 14

John the Baptist said, "I baptize you with water, but the one who is more powerful than me is coming. I'm not worthy to loosen the strap of his sandals. He will baptize you with the Holy Spirit and fire."

Luke 3:16, CEB

SATURDAY · DECEMBER 15

Yes, indeed—God is my salvation.
I trust, I won't be afraid.

Isaiah 12:2, THE MESSAGE

Christ desires to be born in the manger of our hearts. Are the doors of our hearts wide open to receive the shepherds, the Magi, the stray visitors—in a word, humanity? Are they open to receive every person as Christ would receive each one of us?

CATHERINE DE HUECK DOHERTY

© REV. BROTHERJOHN GAUDREAU OEF. ALL RIGHTS RESERVED.

SUNDAY · DECEMBER 16

THIRD SUNDAY OF ADVENT

In that day you will say:
"Give thanks to the LORD, call on
   his name;
 make known among the nations
   what he has done."

Isaiah 12:4, NIV

ZEPHANIAH 3:14-20 · ISAIAH 12:2-6
PHILIPPIANS 4:4-7 · LUKE 3:7-18

MONDAY · DECEMBER 17

Jesus Christ said, "Here I am, to do your will, O God, just as it is written of me in the book of the Law."

Hebrews 10:7, GNT

TUESDAY · DECEMBER 18

You, O Bethlehem Ephrathah,
 are only a small village among all the people of Judah.
Yet a ruler of Israel will come from you,
 one whose origins are from the distant past.

Micah 5:2, NLT

WEDNESDAY · DECEMBER 19

Elizabeth said to Mary, "God has blessed you above all women, and he has blessed the child you carry."
Luke 1:42, CEB

THURSDAY · DECEMBER 20

Mary said,
"My soul magnifies the Lord,
    and my spirit rejoices in God
        my Savior,
for he has looked with favor on the
    lowliness of his servant."
Luke 1:46-48, NRSV

FRIDAY · DECEMBER 21

Mary said, "[God's] faithful love extends age after age to those who fear him."
Luke 1:50, NJB

SATURDAY · DECEMBER 22

Because Jesus Christ did what God wanted him to do, we are all purified from sin by the offering that he made of his own body once and for all.
Hebrews 10:10, GNT

Christmas is the day that holds all time together.

ALEXANDER SMITH

SUNDAY · DECEMBER 23

FOURTH SUNDAY OF ADVENT

Elizabeth said to Mary, "Why am I so honored, that the mother of my Lord should visit me?"

Luke 1:43, NLT

MICAH 5:2-5A · LUKE 1:46B-55
HEBREWS 10:5-10 · LUKE 1:39-45, (46-55)

MONDAY · DECEMBER 24

CHRISTMAS EVE

Sing a new song to the Lord!
   Sing to the Lord, all the world!

Psalm 96:1, GNT

TUESDAY · DECEMBER 25

CHRISTMAS DAY

The angel said to the shepherds, "Today in the town of David a Savior has been born to you; he is Christ the Lord."

Luke 2:11, NIV

WEDNESDAY · DECEMBER 26

You are the people of God; he loved you and chose you for his own.

Colossians 3:12, GNT

THURSDAY · DECEMBER 27

Whatever you do, whether in speech or action, do it all in the name of the Lord Jesus and give thanks to God the Father through him.

Colossians 3:17, CEB

FRIDAY · DECEMBER 28

Clothe yourselves with love, which binds everything together in perfect harmony.

Colossians 3:14, NRSV

SATURDAY · DECEMBER 29

Jesus said to Mary and Joseph, "Why were you looking for me? Didn't you know that I had to be here, dealing with the things of my Father?"

Luke 2:49, THE MESSAGE

I sit on my favorite rock, looking over the brook, to take time away from busy-ness, time to be . . . it's something we all need for our spiritual health, and often we don't take enough of it.

MADELEINE L'ENGLE

SUNDAY · DECEMBER 30

> As the chosen of God . . . be clothed in heartfelt compassion, in generosity and humility, gentleness and patience.
>
> Colossians 3:12, NJB

1 SAMUEL 2:18-20, 26 · PSALM 148
COLOSSIANS 3:12-17 · LUKE 2:41-52

MONDAY · DECEMBER **31**

To every thing there is a season, and a time to every purpose under the heaven: A time to be born, and a time to die.

Ecclesiastes 3:1-2, KJV

ACKNOWLEDGMENTS

January

Ralph Waldo Emerson, in *Wisdom in World Religions: Pathways toward Heaven on Earth* by John Templeton (Philadelphia: Templeton Foundation Press, 2002), 216.

Mother Teresa, *Meditations from a Simple Path* (New York: Ballantine Books, 1996), 53.

Henri J. M. Nouwen, "All Is Grace," *Weavings* 24, no. 3 (May/June 2009), 45.

Father Paul Keenan, *Stages of the Soul: The Path of the Soulful Life* (Lincolnwood, IL: Contemporary Books, 2000), 48.

Macrina Wiederkehr, *Seasons of Your Heart: Prayers and Reflections, Revised and Expanded* (San Francisco: HarperSanFrancisco, 1991), 19.

February

Willa Cather, *Death Comes for the Archbishop* (New York: Vintage, 1971), 50.

Thomas à Kempis, in *A Pattern for Life* (Upper Room Books, 1998), 52–53.

Walter Wangerin Jr., *Reliving the Passion: Meditations on the Suffering, Death, and Resurrection of Jesus as Recorded in Mark* (Grand Rapids, MI: Zondervan Publishing House, 1992), 23.

Paul Wesley Chilcote, *Come, Thou Long-Expected Jesus: Advent and Christmas with Charles Wesley* (Harrisburg, PA: Morehouse Publishing, 2007), 4.

March

David A. Fleming, in *A Maryknoll Book of Inspiration* (Maryknoll, NY: Orbis, 2010), 29.

Gaelic prayer, in *Morning Whispers* (Longwood, FL: Xulon Press, 2010), 3/17/10.

Maria Boulding, *The Coming of God*, 3rd edition (Conception, MO: The Printery House, 2000), 37.

Lauren F. Winner, *Mudhouse Sabbath: An Invitation to a Life of Spiritual Discipline* (Brewster, MA: Paraclete Press, 2003), 90.

April

Anthony de Mello: Writings Selected with an Introduction by William Dych (Maryknoll, NY: Orbis Books, 1999), 57.

Clement of Alexandria, in Martin H. Manswer, comp., *The Westminster Collection of Christian Quotations* (Louisville, KY: Westminster John Knox Press, 2001).

Mary Lou Kownacki, *A Monk in the Inner City: The ABCs of a Spiritual Journey* (Maryknoll, NY: Orbis Books, 2008).

Elizabeth J. Canham, *Heart Whispers: Benedictine Wisdom for Today* (Nashville, TN: Upper Room Books, 1999), 63.

Michael Downey, *Altogether Gift: A Trinitarian Spirituality* (Maryknoll, NY: Orbis Books, 2000), .

MAY
Brother Lawrence, *The Practice of the Presence of God* (Orleans, MA: Paraclete Press, 1985), 76.

Grace Imathiu, from a tagline in an email March 5, 2010.

Rubem Alves, in *Formations: Learner's Study Guide, January-April 2009* (Macon, GA: Smyth & Helwys Publishing), 109.

Stephen V. Doughty with Marjorie J. Thompson, *The Way of Discernment, Participant's Book* (Nashville, TN: Upper Room Books, 2008), 26.

JUNE
Daniel Wolpert, *Creating a Life with God: The Call of Ancient Prayer Practices* (Nashville, TN: Upper Room Books, 2003).

Marjorie J. Thompson and Stephen D. Bryant, *Exploring the Way, Leader's Guide* (Nashville, TN: Upper Room Books: 2005), 44.

Peter Abelard, in *The Letters of Abelard and Heloise* (Harmondsworth: Penguin, 1974), 270–71.

Beatrice of Nazareth, "On Seven Ways of Divine Love," http://dspace.dial.pipex.com/town/avenue/pd49/pockets/people/holylove.html. Text copyright© Andy Anderson, 1999-2001.

JULY
Brother Lawrence, *The Practice of the Presence of God* (Brewster, MA: Paraclete Press, 1985), 86.

John of the Cross, *Dark Night of the Soul* (Radford, VA: Wilder Publications, 2008), 111.

Helen Julian CSF, *The Road to Emmaus: Companions for the Journey through Lent* (Nashville, TN: Upper Room Books, 2006), 95.

Norman Borlaug, "The Green Revolution: For Bread and Peace," *Science and Public Affairs* 27, no. 6 (June, 1971), 7.

J. David Muyskens, *Forty Days to a Closer Walk with God: The Practice of Centering Prayer* (Nashville: Upper Room Books, 2007), 58.

AUGUST
Henri J. M. Nouwen, in *A Maryknoll Book of Inspiration* (Maryknoll, NY: Orbis, 2010), 319.

Daniel Wolpert, *Creating a Life with God: The Call of Ancient Prayer Practices* (Nashville, TN: Upper Room Books, 2003).

Meeting God in Scripture: Entering the New Testament, Participant's Workbook (Nashville, TN: Upper Room Books, 2008), 74.

Joseph R. Veneroso, in *A Maryknoll Book of Inspiration* (Maryknoll, NY: Orbis, 2010), 363.

September

Mother Teresa, *Meditations from a Simple Path* (New York: Ballantine Books, 1996), 87.

Ernesto Cardenal, in *Alive Now* (May/June 2004): 4.

Christopher Maricle, *The Jesus Priorities: 8 Essential Habits* (Nashville, TN: Upper Room Books, 2007), 18.

Francois Fénelon, in *Teachings of the Christian Mystics* (Boston: Shambhala Publications, 1998), 86.

Nelson Mandela, in *A Maryknoll Book of Inspiration* (Maryknoll, NY: Orbis, 2010), 313.

October

Jim Forest, in *A Maryknoll Book of Inspiration* (Maryknoll, NY: Orbis, 2010), 316.

Archbishop Rowan Williams, from *Sojourners, Voice and Verse* 02/01/11.

Patricia F. Wilson, *Quiet Spaces* (Nashville, TN: Upper Room Books, 2002), 89.

G. K. Chesterton, in *A Maryknoll Book of Inspiration* (Maryknoll, NY: Orbis, 2010), 45.

November

Lynne M. Babb, *Sabbath Keeping: Finding Freedom in the Rhythms of Rest* (Downers Grove, IL: InterVarsity Press, 2005), 11.

Steve Harper, *Talking in the Dark: Praying When Life Doesn't Make Sense* (Nashville, TN: Upper Room Books, 2007), 85.

Anne Lamott, *Traveling Mercies* (New York: Pantheon, 1999).

Lynne M. Babb, *Sabbath Keeping*, 77.

December

Frederick Buechner, *The Alphabet of Grace* (New York: Seabury, 1970), 103.

Phillips Brooks, "O Little Town of Bethlehem," in *The United Methodist Hymnal* (Nashville, TN: The United Methodist Publishing House, 1989), no. 230.

Catherine de Hueck Doherty, *Donkey Bells: Advent and Christmas with Catherine Doherty*, comp. Mary Bazzett (Combermere, Ontario: Madonna House Publications, 2000), 55.

Alexander Smith, in *Alive Now* (November/December 2004): 4.

Madeleine L'Engle, *Walking on Water: Reflections on Faith and Art* (New York: North Point Press, 1995), 12.